Iolanda Bolduc • Jean Sasso

THE NEW CLUES TO ENGLISH

English as a Second Language   Second Cycle Elementary

STUDENT BOOK
B

LES ÉDITIONS
CEC
Une compagnie de Quebecor Media

9001, boul. Louis-H.-La Fontaine, Anjou (Québec) Canada H1J 2C5
Téléphone : 514-351-6010 • Télécopieur : 514-351-3534

Managing Director, ESL:
Leena M. Sandblom

Production Manager:
Danielle Latendresse

Project Editor:
Lori Schubert

Cover and page design:
Matteau Parent graphisme et communication inc.
Marc Gaudreault, art director
Mélanie Chalifour, cover designer
Sylvie Bouchard, page designer

Illustrations:
Valérie Morency
Arianne Turgeon
Caroline Dion

Gouvernement du Québec – Programme de crédit d'impôt
pour l'édition de livres – Gestion SODEC

© 2001, Les éditions CEC inc.
9001, boul. Louis-H.-La Fontaine
Anjou (Québec) H1J 2C5

Dépôt légal,
Bibliothèque nationale du Québec,
2e trimestre 2001

Legal deposit,
National Library of Canada,
2nd quarter 2001

ISBN 978-2-7617-1721-2

Printed in Canada
5 6 7 8 9 14 13 12 11 10

ABOUT THE AUTHORS

Iolanda Bolduc taught English as a second language (ESL) at
the primary level for many years and, prior to retirement, was
the pedagogical consultant at the former Commission scolaire
de l'Eau-Vive (Longueuil). She is the author of *Jigsaw One*,
Jigsaw Two and co-author of *Kaleidoscope* and the All-Star
Series of activity books, as well as the first edition of *Clues to
English* for Grade 4 and 5 students. She pioneered the teaching
of intensive English at the former Commission scolaire
Greenfield Park.

Jean Sasso was a co-author of the first edition of *Clues to
English* for Grade 4 and Grade 6 students and the All-Star Series
of activity books. Much of her work was retained for *The New
Clues to English*, Second Cycle, Book B. After a long career
teaching ESL, Jean is now enjoying her retirement.

ACKNOWLEDGEMENTS

The authors wish to express their thanks to the whole team
at CEC Publishing for their steadfast commitment to this series
and their role in bringing the material to fruition. Heartfelt
thanks go to Leena M. Sandblom for her direction, leadership
and constant support on the project, to Lori Schubert for
her excellent editorial work, unfailing good humour and
encouragement, to the whole team at Matteau Parent for their
fine graphic work, and to Leon Aronson, Robert Leblanc, Gerry
Leduc, Trevor Jones, Rosie Emery, and Peter John Bailey for
their entertaining songs.

They also wish to thank the participants of the focus groups
held in Montreal in the fall of 2000 for their invaluable advice.
Their insights helped to make *The New Clues to English* what
it is today.

Special thanks go to Donald for his understanding, patience
and encouragement from start to finish.

SOURCES

Page 96: photograph by F. Lepine/Reflexion Phototheque,
Page 102: Photographs: Dog sledding: Yann/Guichaoua/
Publiphoto; Snow sculptures: D. Vayer/Publiphoto; Skating:
P. Andrews/Publiphoto; Sleigh ride: P. Adam/Publiphoto;
Ice fishing: I. Bolduc; Barrel jumping: M. F. Coallier/
Publiphoto, **Page 108:** photograph A courtesy of Jean Sasso;
photograph B: Y. Beaulieu/Publiphoto; photograph C: P.
Jenson/Reflexion Phototheque; photograph D courtesy
of Ontario Tourism Marketing Partnership; photograph E:
Hattenberger/Publiphoto; photograph F: S. Naiman/Reflexion
Phototheque, Page **115:** Photograph of children in pageant
courtesy of the Kativik School Board, photographs of igloo-
building contest courtesy of the Quebec Ministry of Culture
and Communications, **Page 117-124:** "It's School Time" and
"Colours and Shapes", music by Gerry Leduc, lyrics by Robert
Leblanc; "The Robot Song", music and lyrics by Trevor Jones;
"This Old Man", "A-Hunting We Will Go" and "We Wish You
a Merry Christmas", traditional; "It's Wintertime", lyrics by
Iolanda Bolduc; "The Recycling Boogie", Music by Rosie Emery
and Peter John Bailey, lyrics by Rosie Emery; "Up on the
Rooftop", music and lyrics by Benjamin R. Hanby.

CONTENTS

HELP STATION

What's your name?

ask

Robert

answer

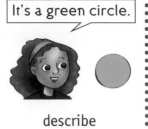
It's a green circle.

describe

draw

find

learn

listen

look

make

match

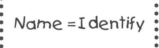
Name = Identify

name

point

read

share

Your turn

take turns

tell

use

write

Pair activity

Group activity

Class activity

Listening activity

Reading activity

four

Writing activity

Welcome Back

A new school year, a new start

Let's find out what you remember.

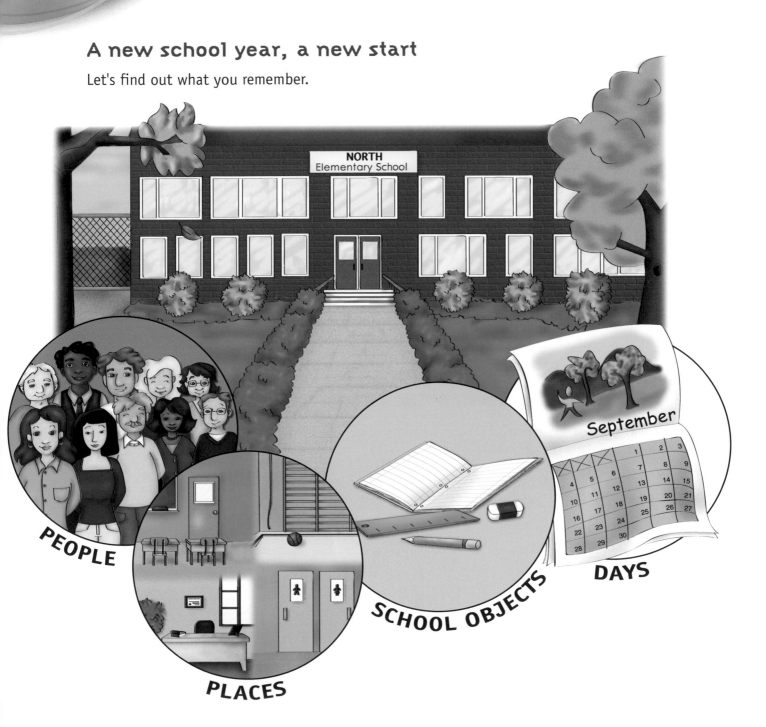

PEOPLE

PLACES

SCHOOL OBJECTS

DAYS

- Form a group.
- Make a list for each category: *people, places, school objects and days*.
- Some of the information is in this unit.

A new book, new people

This girl and boy are twins. Who are they?

- Look in this unit to answer these questions.

1. What are their names?
2. What is the name of their school?
3. What class are they in?
4. What is the name of their teacher?

5. What is his name?
   Look for the answer in Unit 2.

6. What is her name?
   Look for the answer in Unit 2.

7. What is its name?
   Look for the answer in Unit 3.

- Compare answers with a partner.

Now let's find out about Kim and Kevin's special
"Welcome Back" school activity.

① Show and Tell

Kim and Kevin McKenzie go to North Elementary School.
They are in Elementary 4. Mr. Palardi is their teacher.
It's the first week of school and the class is having a Show and Tell.
The twins have something special to show the class.

GETTiNG READY TO LiSTEN AND READ

1 Look at the pictures on page 8.
 • What are the twins going to show the class?
2 Look at the pictures and text on pages 8 to 11.
 • Find one key word for each picture.

Now listen and read along.

Kim and Kevin are introducing their little brother to the class.

> This is our brother. His name is Robert. He's four years old.

> Hi.

> He's in pre-kindergarten. Say "Hi," Robert.

> Hi, Robert.

> He's cute.

> Hello.

Robert has fun in the classroom.

Mr. Palardi gives him some colouring pencils and paper.

He draws some pictures and shows them to the class.

> This is my dog. Rusty is eight years old.

> This is my cat. Her name is Princess. She's twelve years old.

> This is my house. I live on Laurier Street.

At recess, the twins take Robert around the school.

They introduce him to the principal, Mr. Robbins.

They introduce him to the secretary, Doris Thompson.

They introduce him to Bob, the janitor,

and to Miss Ling, the nurse.

They introduce him to some of the teachers, too.

Hi, Mrs. Goulet. This is our little brother, Robert.

Well, hello, Robert. How are you?

Fine, thank you.

How old are you?

I'm four.

Do you go to school?

I'm in pre-kindergarten.

Do you like school?

Yes.

Then the children go out to play.
Robert plays ball with the Elementary 1 students.
Kim and Kevin play with their friends.

The bell rings. Recess is finished. Robert follows the Elementary 1 students into the school. Kim and Kevin look for him.

They look in the yard.
Robert is not there.

They look in their classroom.
Robert is not there.

They look in the nurse's office.
Robert is not there.

They look in the washrooms.
Robert is not there.

They go to the secretary's office.
Robert is not there.

They go to the principal's office.
Robert is not there.

They go to the teachers' room.
Robert is not there.

They even go to the Elementary 1 classroom.
Robert is not there.

Finally they look in the library. Robert is there. He is sitting on the floor, looking at a book. Kim and Kevin are happy. So is Robert.

 STOP

AFTER LISTENING AND READING

1 All about Kim and Kevin's brother
 - Answer the questions.
   a) What is his name?
   b) How old is he?
   c) Does he go to school?

2 Kim and Kevin introduce their brother to the school personnel.
 - Match the occupations and names.
   a) principal
   b) secretary
   c) janitor
   d) nurse
   e) Kim and Kevin's teacher

   1. Miss Ling
   2. Mr. Robbins
   3. Mr. Palardi
   4. Bob
   5. Doris Thompson

3 Name three things Robert likes to do.
 - Find the information in the unit.

4 Compare answers.

② Yes/No questions

DETECTIVE DAN'S CLUE

Yes/No Questions	Answers
Is Robert in the gymnasium? ⟶	**No**, he **is not**.
Is he in the classroom? ⟶	**No**, he **isn't**.
Is he in the library? ⟶	**Yes**, he **is**.

- Look at the illustrations. Answer the questions.
- Use **she** for a female and **he** for a male.

1 Is Kim in the classroom?

2 Is she in the schoolyard?

3 Is Kevin in the gymnasium?

4 Is he in the washroom?

5 Is Mr. Robbins in his office?

6 Is he in the teachers' room?

7 Is Mrs. Thompson in the library?

8 Is she in the nurse's office?

- Take turns asking the Yes/No questions.
- Listen to your partner's answer. Is it correct?

3 Asking for permission in class

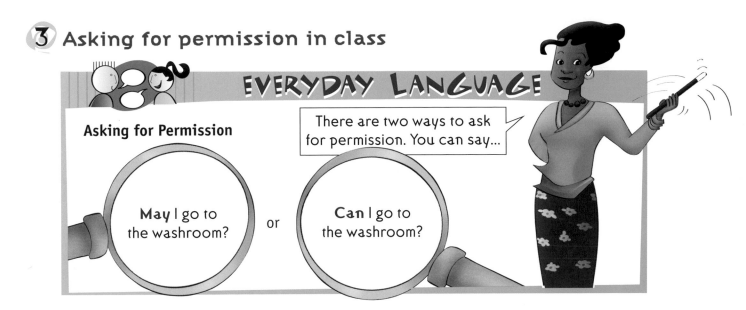

EVERYDAY LANGUAGE

Asking for Permission

There are two ways to ask for permission. You can say...

May I go to the washroom?

or

Can I go to the washroom?

1 Identify the pictures that show the key words.

KEY WORDS

copybooks   door   board   wastebasket   school bag

A   B   C   D   E

2 Listen to the students. Find the correct picture.

3 Match the action words with the correct pictures.

KEY WORDS

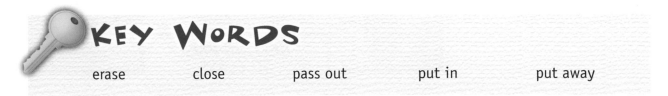

erase   close   pass out   put in   put away

4 • Practice asking for permission. Use the pictures.
     • Identify other things you have to ask for permission to do.

Play Getting Back to Class

1 Look at the board game. Your teacher will give it to you.
- Name the different rooms.
- Name these school objects.

A

B

C

D

E

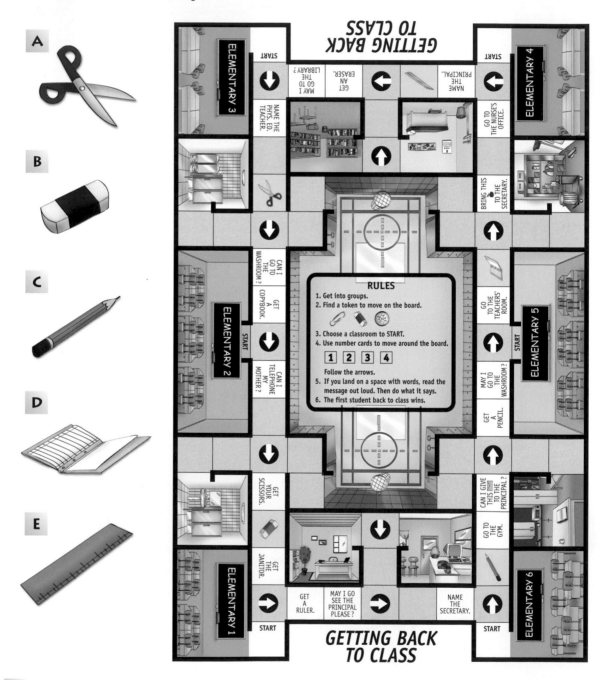

GETTING BACK TO CLASS

ELEMENTARY 3 — START

NAME THE PHYS. ED. TEACHER.

MAY I GO TO THE LIBRARY?

GET AN ERASER.

NAME THE PRINCIPAL.

START — ELEMENTARY 4

GO TO THE NURSE'S OFFICE.

BRING THIS TO THE SECRETARY.

CAN I GO TO THE WASHROOM?

GET A COPYBOOK.

ELEMENTARY 2 — START

CAN I TELEPHONE MY MOTHER?

RULES
1. Get into groups.
2. Find a token to move on the board.
3. Choose a classroom to START.
4. Use number cards to move around the board.

`1` `2` `3` `4`

Follow the arrows.
5. If you land on a space with words, read the message out loud. Then do what it says.
6. The first student back to class wins.

GO TO THE TEACHERS' ROOM.

START — ELEMENTARY 5

MAY I GO TO THE WASHROOM?

GET A PENCIL.

GET YOUR SCISSORS.

GET THE JANITOR.

CAN I GIVE THIS TO THE PRINCIPAL?

GO TO THE GYM.

ELEMENTARY 1 — START

GET A RULER.

MAY I GO SEE THE PRINCIPAL PLEASE?

NAME THE SECRETARY.

START — ELEMENTARY 6

GETTING BACK TO CLASS

2 Do you understand the messages?

3 Do you understand the rules?

4 Play the game.

TIME OUT

Where's the snake?

Listen.

My snake is missing. Where's my snake?

A snake! All right. O.K. Let's be calm. Look around the...

A

B

C

D

E

F

G

Asking for permission

Listen.

Can I...?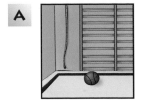

May I...?

A

B

C

D

E

F

G

H

I

J

Ask for permission
• Use the pictures.

How are you doing?

In this unit we reviewed...

UNIT 2
Magic Mandy's Tricks

Mandy likes to do card tricks.
Her assistant Sue picks a card.
Mandy has to guess the card.

- Look at the cards.
  What does Mandy need to know?

Your teacher will do the trick and teach it to you.
- First review the colours and shapes.

① A review of colours

• Name the colours.

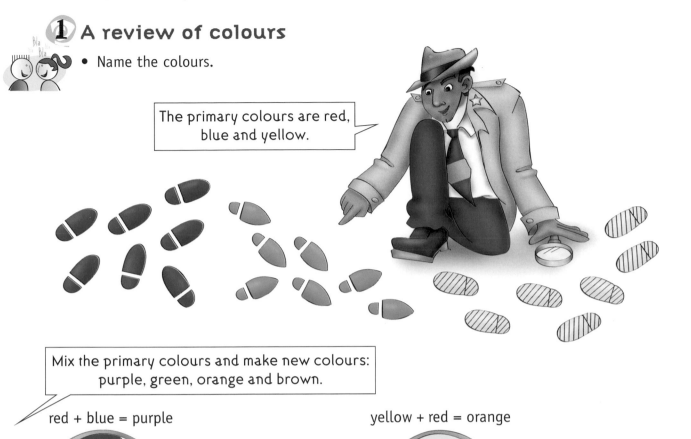

The primary colours are red, blue and yellow.

Mix the primary colours and make new colours: purple, green, orange and brown.

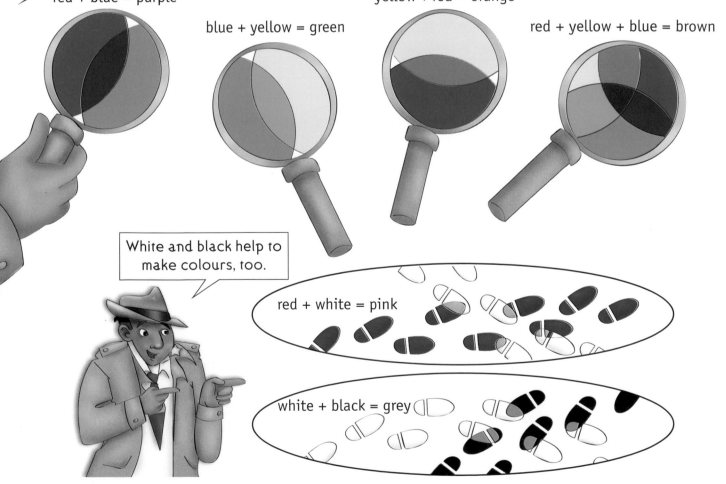

red + blue = purple

blue + yellow = green

yellow + red = orange

red + yellow + blue = brown

White and black help to make colours, too.

red + white = pink

white + black = grey

2 A review of shapes

- Listen to Detective Dan.
- Identify the shapes.

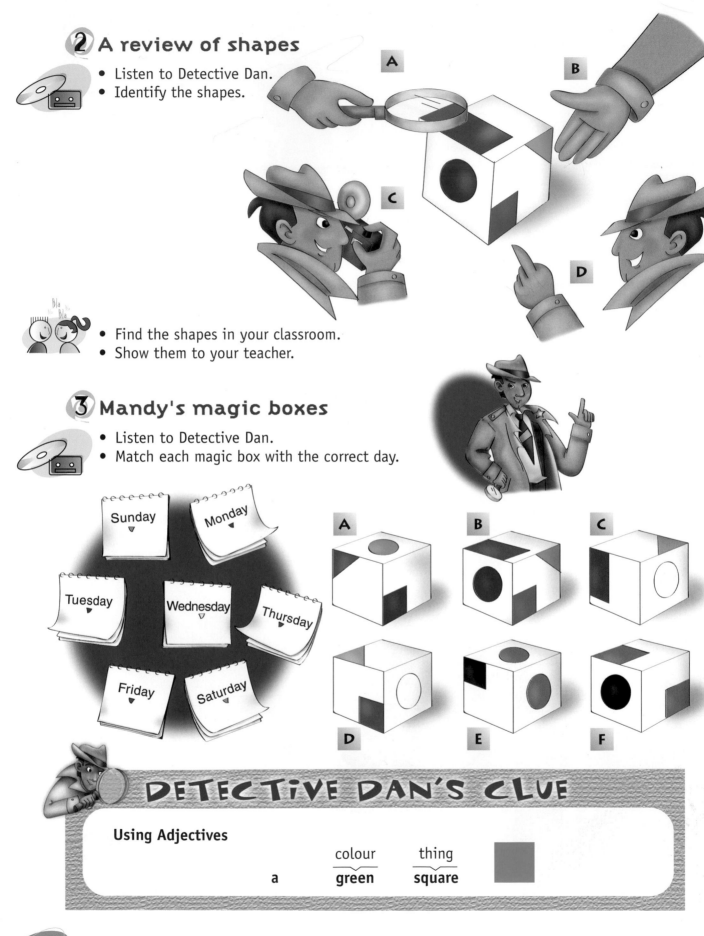

- Find the shapes in your classroom.
- Show them to your teacher.

3 Mandy's magic boxes

- Listen to Detective Dan.
- Match each magic box with the correct day.

Sunday   Monday

Tuesday   Wednesday   Thursday

Friday   Saturday

A   B   C

D   E   F

DETECTIVE DAN'S CLUE

Using Adjectives

	colour	thing	
a	**green**	**square**	

④ Magic Mandy's scarf tricks

- Watch Mandy do her scarf tricks.

KEY WORDS

trick   scarf

First,
I pull out one scarf.
It's yellow.

Then, I pull out two
scarves - a purple
scarf and a pink scarf.

Then I pull out three scarves - a
white scarf, a blue scarf and
a black scarf. This is fun!

- Now listen to Mandy.
  What scarf trick is she doing?

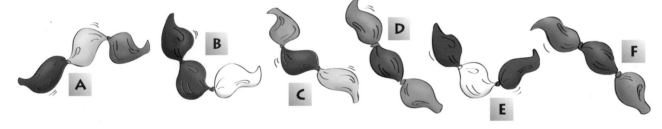

⑤ Magic Mandy's colourful clothes

Mandy has a new jacket.
It has a green square and
a green circle.

- Describe the other shapes.

- Colour a new jacket for Mandy.
- Describe it to a classmate.

This is Mandy's
new jacket.

Do Mandy's Card Trick

1 Magic Mandy and Sue are doing the card trick.
* Look at the pictures and read the text.

It is red.

It is a red circle.

Correct.

Fantastic!

2 Watch your teacher do the trick.
* Find the secret of the trick.

3 Learn how to do the trick.
* Your teacher will explain.

HAVE FUN!

TiME OUT

Coloured shapes

Listen.

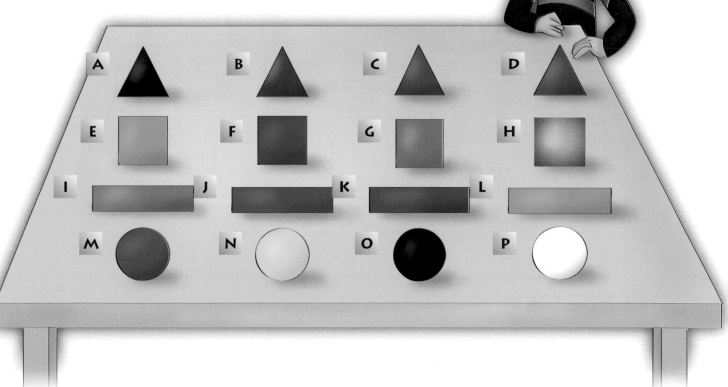

Describing things

Describe things to a partner. See if your partner can find them.

- Describe three shapes on page 16.
- Describe one of Mandy's boxes on page 18.
- Describe one of Mandy's scarf tricks on page 19.

After this unit I can...

How are *you* doing?

PROJECT Fun with Colours and Shapes

① Connection line

I have a green triangle.

I have a red circle.

I have a red triangle.

I have a blue circle.

I have a...

Do you understand how to play this game?
• Look at the pictures. Read the text.
• Play the game with your classmates.

② Matching up

Do you have an orange heart?

Do you have a yellow star?

No. My turn.

Yes, I do. Here it is.

• Play this game with your classmates.

③ Art

- What is Annie's picture?
- What is Denny's picture?
- Make a picture using coloured paper and shapes.

YOUR PROJECT

What can you do with colours and shapes? Any ideas?

- Talk about your ideas.

- Prepare the activity. Share the work.
  1. What material do you need?
  2. What are the instructions?

- Explain and demonstrate your activity to your classmates.

Let's...

HAVE FUN!

Robots at School

This is a special week at North Elementary School. There is a robot exhibition in the school. Robots are visiting for one week. Mr. Robbins, the principal, is introducing the robots to the students.

> Now let's meet them. From left to right, they are Kiki, Chip, Mico and Tiny.

> Error. My name is Mico. My model number is KS 58-2. Tiny is shorter.

- How many robots are visiting?
- What are their names?
- Which robot do you like best?
- Tell a classmate three things about how it looks.
- Look at page 30.
  What activity are you going to do at the end of this unit?
  What do you need to learn in English to do this activity?

① Model numbers

• Learn all the parts of the body.

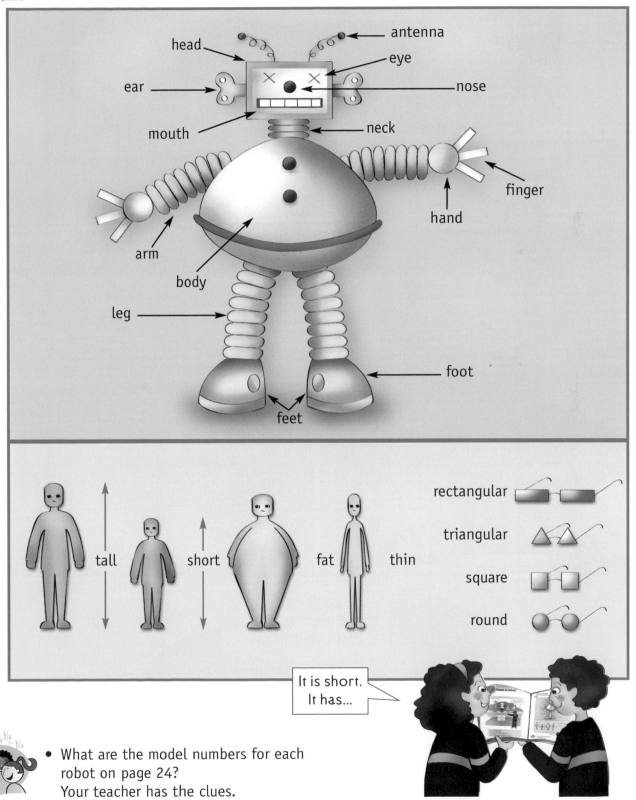

antenna
head
eye
ear
nose
mouth
neck
finger
hand
arm
body
leg
foot
feet

tall   short   fat   thin

rectangular
triangular
square
round

It is short.
It has...

• What are the model numbers for each
robot on page 24?
Your teacher has the clues.

②In the classroom

At ten o'clock, Mico arrives in Mr. Palardi's classroom.

START

Wow!

Well, kids,
here is our special guest.

Look.

Can you
spell your name?

Can you
write?

Yes.

Yes, I can.
M...I...C...O.

Mico, go to the board...
Take a piece of chalk...
Write your name.

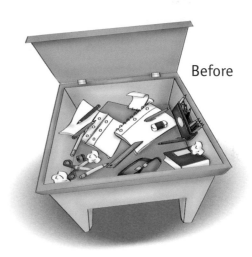

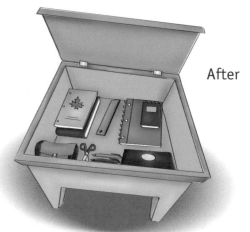

Before

After

1 What can Mico do?

2 Name the objects in Kim's desk.

3 What can Mico do?

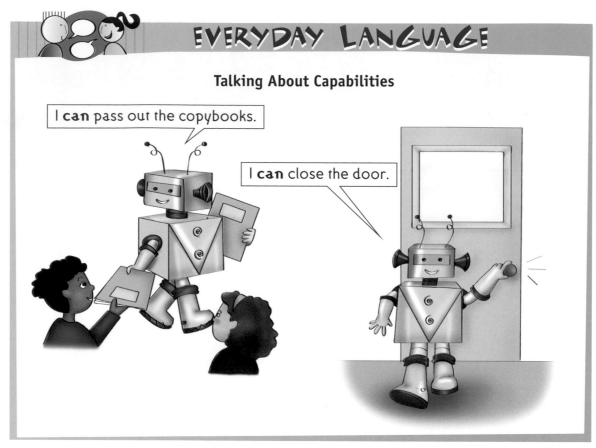

EVERYDAY LANGUAGE

Talking About Capabilities

I **can** pass out the copybooks.

I **can** close the door.

• Listen. Find the correct picture.

④ More talk

DETECTIVE DAN'S CLUE

The Pronoun "It"

It = thing

The Pronoun "I"

I = myself

- Look at the pictures on pages 26 to 28.
  1. Tell your partner what Mico can do.
  2. Tell your partner what you can do in class.

⑤ Can you...?

EVERYDAY LANGUAGE

Asking About Capabilities:
Can...?

Can you walk to school?

Yes, I **can**.

No, I **can't**. It's too far.
I take the school bus.

- Answer the questions.
  1. Can you spell your name in English?
  2. Can you count from one to twenty-five in English?
  3. Can you stand on one foot for one minute?

Have A Class Robot Exhibition

1 Design a robot.
- Use different objects for the parts of the body.
  Examples:

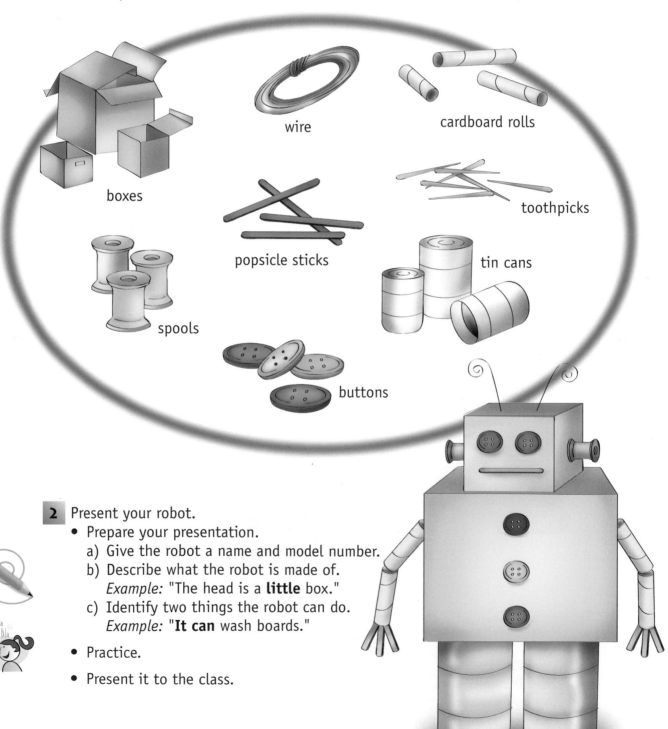

boxes

wire

cardboard rolls

popsicle sticks

toothpicks

spools

tin cans

buttons

2 Present your robot.
- Prepare your presentation.
  a) Give the robot a name and model number.
  b) Describe what the robot is made of.
     Example: "The head is a **little** box."
  c) Identify two things the robot can do.
     Example: "**It can** wash boards."

- Practice.

- Present it to the class.

TiME OUT

The robot exhibit

Listen.

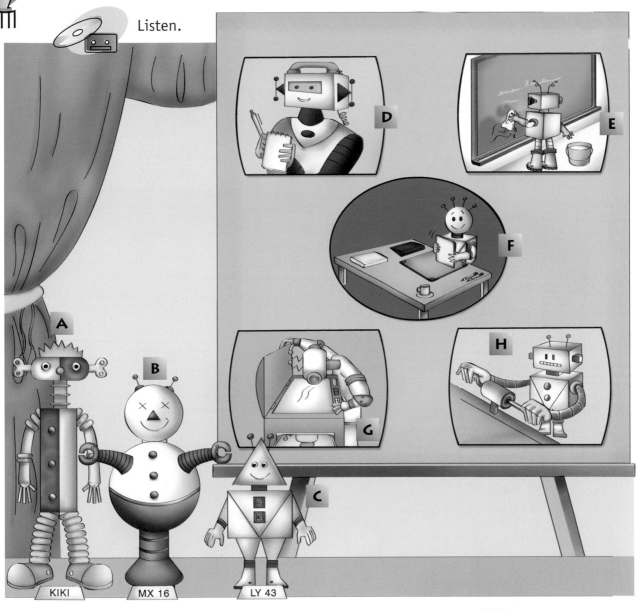

Describe one robot to a classmate.

It is...
It has...

After this unit I can...

How are *you* doing?

UNIT 4
Mico's Fantastic Adventures

One day in school Kevin decides to write a story about Mico.

This is how the story begins....

Hey, Mico. What are these buttons? Let's try 1... 2... 8... 7.

Do not push the buttons. Do not...

HELP!

Stories are fun. Stories are creative.

- What happens to Mico in Kevin's story?
- What are you going to do at the end of this unit?

STORY TiME

Enjoy a story. Your teacher will help you.

GETTING READY TO LISTEN AND READ

1 How many adventures does Mico have?

2 In his adventures, Mico meets these people.
Can you identify each person?

princess

queen

wizard

prince

king

knight

3 Look at page 34.

- Where is Mico?
- Find these key words.
  Do you know what they mean?
- Listen.

KEY WORDS

| century | size | rock |
| powder | shape | flat |

4 It's time for Mico's adventures.

- Look at pages 35 to 38.
- Find the pictures for the key words.

Now listen and read along.

Mico's fantastic adventure begins.

Mico leaves the wizard.
He has some adventures.

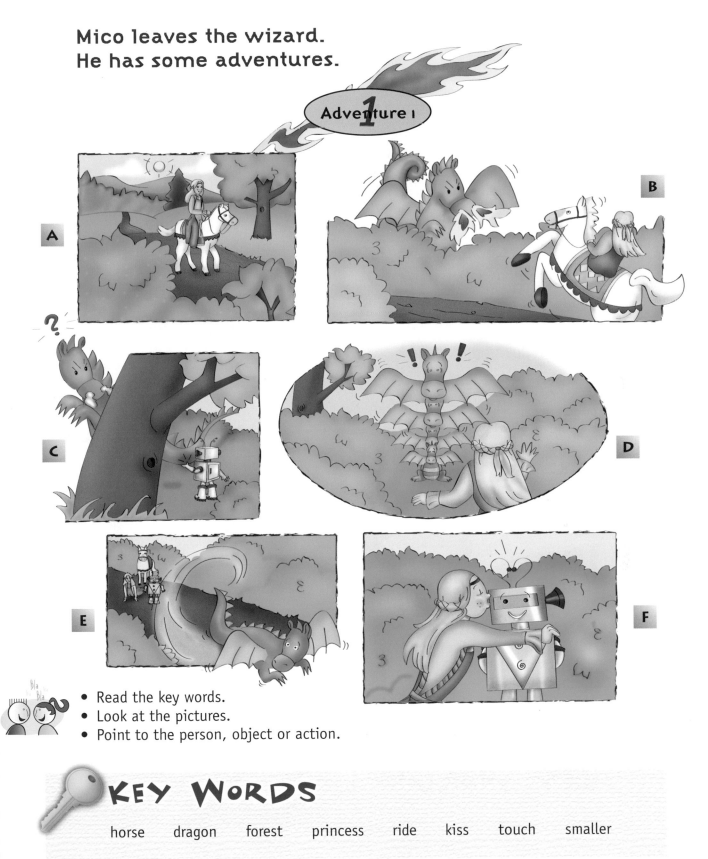

Adventure 1

- Read the key words.
- Look at the pictures.
- Point to the person, object or action.

KEY WORDS

horse   dragon   forest   princess   ride   kiss   touch   smaller

- Listen.

A

B

C

D

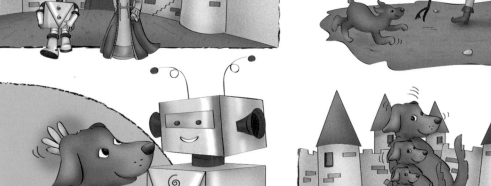

E

F

- Read the key words.
- Look at the pictures.
- Point to the person, object or action.

KEY WORDS

castle   courtyard   king   queen   prince   pat   play   bigger

- Listen.

Adventure 3

A

B

C

D

E

F

- Read the key words.
- Look at the pictures.
- Point to the person, object or action.

KEY WORDS

schoolroom	geography	lesson	map	earth	round

- Listen.

A

B

C

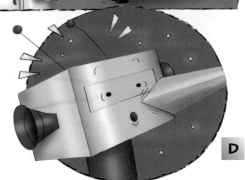

D

E

F

- Read the key words.
- Look at the pictures.
- Point to the person, object or action.

 KEY WORDS

knight   sword   walk   taller   smaller

- Listen.

The next day at four o'clock...

It is time to go back, Mico.

Goodbye, Princess.
Goodbye, Waldo.
Thanks for everything.

AFTER LISTENING AND READING

1 Show your partner your favourite adventure. Describe it.

2 Listen to Mico's adventures again. This time they are out of order. Identify each adventure.

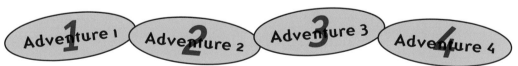

Adventure 1   Adventure 2   Adventure 3   Adventure 4

3 Mico has an adventure with the cook.
Listen to your teacher.

DETECTIVE DAN'S CLUE

Using the Present Tense

He
She } verb + **s**
It

Examples:

He run**s** to the castle.

She eat**s** chocolate cake.

It get**s** smaller.

Things the Princess Does

- Read the key words.
- Complete the sentences below.

KEY WORDS

eats	listens	pats
plays	rides	runs
	walks	

A. Princess Emily _____ in the castle.

B. She _____ in the forest.

C. She _____ with Prince Paul.

D. She _____ with the family.

E. She _____ Ruby.

F. She _____ to her teacher.

G. She _____ a horse.

Make a Mini-Booklet

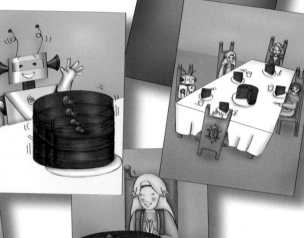

1 Make the mini-booklet.
Your teacher will explain.

2 Cut out the text for each page.

3 Glue the texts into the mini-booklet.

4 Practice reading the story with a partner.

5 Read the mini-booklet to your parents.

EVERYDAY LANGUAGE

Asking for Help

"Help me, please."

"I need help."

"Can you help me, please?"

"I don't understand."

Marvellous Mico

 Listen.

B

A

C

H

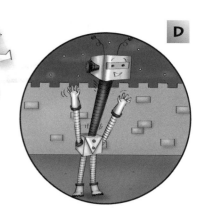

D

G

F

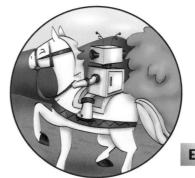

E

ME OUT

Happy together!

Listen to your teacher.

1. In a land far away, there is a big castle.

2. The king and queen and their daughter, Princess Anna, live in the castle. They are happy together.

3. The royal family is protected by a brave knight.

4. One day, a prince named Michael comes to visit.

5. A fierce dragon attacks the castle.

6. The knight and the courageous prince fight the dragon.

7. The dragon runs to the forest.

8. Everyone celebrates the victory with a nice supper.

9. Princess Anna and Prince Michael are very happy together.

How are *you* doing?

After this unit I can...

**PROJECT**

Writing a Mini-Adventure About Your Robot

① Getting ready to write

- Look at the information on this page.
- Talk about your ideas.

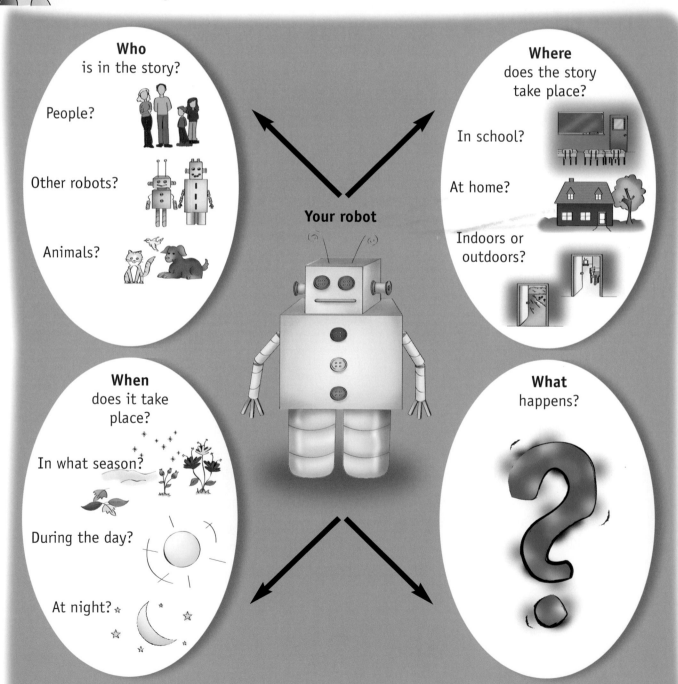

Who is in the story?

People?

Other robots?

Animals?

Where does the story take place?

In school?

At home?

Indoors or outdoors?

Your robot

When does it take place?

In what season?

During the day?

At night?

What happens?

② Writing your first draft

- Write your first draft.

  1. Write six sentences –
     one for each page in the booklet.

  2. Write a title for your story.

- Read your first draft.

  1. Check the story for logical order.

  2. Check your sentences for capital letters and
     correct punctuation. See the rules on page 130.

  3. Check for correct spelling.

  4. Exchange first drafts with a classmate.

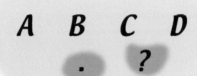

A B C D

. ?

YOUR PROJECT

1 Make your mini-booklet.

- Prepare the mini-booklet.
- Write the title on the front page.
- Write the story.
- Draw a picture on every page.

2 Share your mini-booklet.

- Practice reading your story.
- Read your story to the class.
- Read your story to your parents.

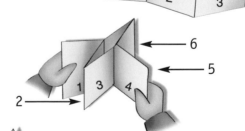

The McKenzie Family

This is Kevin and Kim's family.
Can you identify the different members of the family?
Use the key words.

KEY WORDS

mother	father	sister
brother	cat	dog

In this unit you will present your family. What information do you need for the presentation?

- Look through the unit.
- Make a list.

① Meet the McKenzie Family

GETTING READY TO LISTEN AND READ

- Find the name and age of each person.

Now listen and read along.

 START

Meet our family. Here's our mother. Her name is Carol. She's 38.

This is our father. His name is Steve. He's 37.

We have a little brother, Robert. He's four.

Our big sister is thirteen. Her name is Lynne.

There are six people in our family.

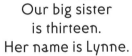

Don't forget our dog Rusty and our cat Princess. They're our family, too.

 STOP

② Age = number

EVERYDAY LANGUAGE

Asking About Age:
How old are you?

Four.

Different ways to answer the question:

Nine years old.

I'm thirteen.

- Count from 1 to 10.
- Learn these numbers.

11 eleven   **12** twelve   **13** thirteen   **14** fourteen   **15** fifteen

16 sixteen   **17** seventeen   **18** eighteen   **19** nineteen   **20** twenty

30 thirty   **40** forty   **50** fifty   **60** sixty

70 seventy   **80** eighty   **90** ninety   **100** one hundred

- Practice saying these numbers.

33   56   79

41   82   25

97   64   38

Your family presentation...
Do you know the age of each member of your family?
- Write down the information.

③ More about the McKenzies

GETTING READY TO LISTEN AND READ

1   Look at the pictures on pages 49 and 50.
- What is the new information about the McKenzie family?

2   Look at the text.
- Find the key words for each picture.

> Now listen and read along.

START Here is information about what the members of the McKenzie family do and what they like.
• Listen to Kevin and Kim.

Dad is a mechanic. He fixes trucks and cars.

He likes to play hockey...

...and go fishing.

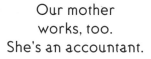

Our mother works, too. She's an accountant.

She likes aerobics.

Robert is in pre-kindergarten. He likes to play all day.

Lynne's our older sister. She goes to high school.

She likes basketball...

...and music.

Kevin and I like to climb trees...

...and play video games...

That's our family.

...and you know that we go to North Elementary.

STOP

AFTER LISTENING AND READING

- Name the occupation of each person in the McKenzie family.
- Name the activities they like.

Your family presentation...
Do you know the occupation of each person in your family?
Do you know one activity each person likes?
- Write down the information.

She = female
He = male

4 Detective Dan's questions

DETECTIVE DAN'S CLUE

Her name is Kim McKenzie.

My name is Dan Martin.

His name is Kevin.

• Take turns answering the questions.

What's his name?

What's her name?

A

B

What's her name?
What's her occupation?

C

What's his name?
What's his occupation?

D

What's her name?
What's her occupation?

E

What's my name?
What's my occupation?

F

5 The McKenzie family tree

DETECTIVE DAN'S CLUE

This is my mother.
Her name is Lily.
She's 65.

This is my father.
His name is Benjamin.
He's 71.

We use **she** for a female.

We use **he** for a male.

- Take turns pointing to the grandparents.
- Say the name and age of Kim and Kevin's two grandmothers and grandfathers.

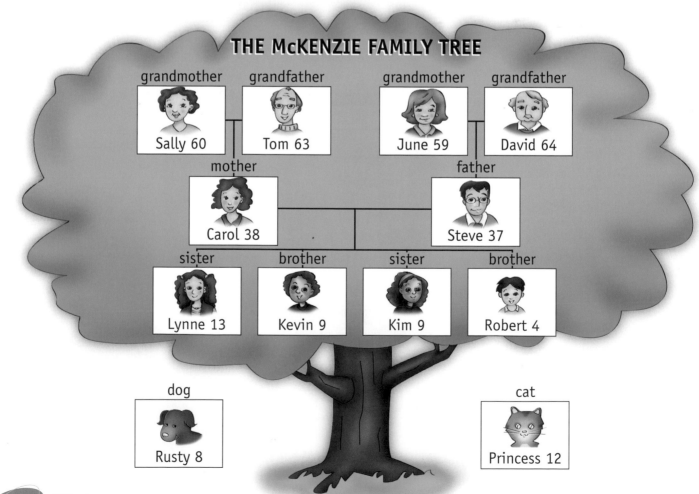

THE McKENZIE FAMILY TREE

grandmother	grandfather	grandmother	grandfather
Sally 60	Tom 63	June 59	David 64

mother — Carol 38

father — Steve 37

sister	brother	sister	brother
Lynne 13	Kevin 9	Kim 9	Robert 4

dog
Rusty 8

cat
Princess 12

Talk About Your Family

1 Make a family tree.

2 Write about one member of your family.
* Tell this person's **name**, **age** and **occupation**.
* Name one **activity** this person likes to do.

Examples:

play chess   work on a computer   talk on the phone   ski

3 Share this information with your classmates.

TIME OUT

Kim's family

Listen.

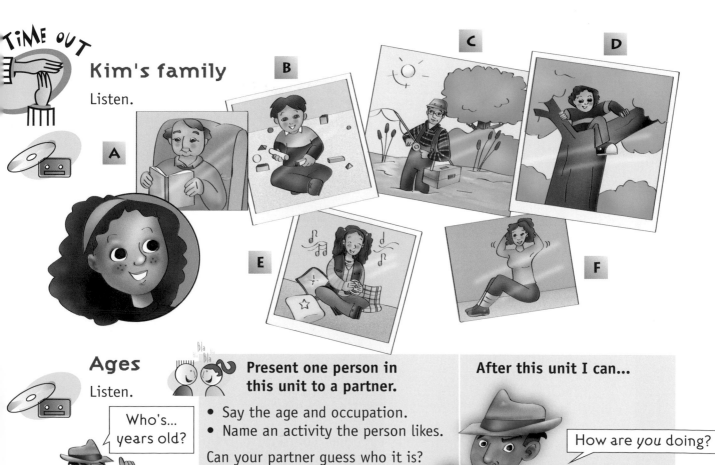

Ages

Listen.

Who's... years old?

Present one person in this unit to a partner.

* Say the age and occupation.
* Name an activity the person likes.

Can your partner guess who it is?

After this unit I can...

How are *you* doing?

A New Friend

Kim has a new friend. Her name is Amy.
Amy is a student at North Elementary School.

- Look at the picture.
  Where are Kim and Amy?
  What are they doing?

In this unit you will prepare information about yourself to give to a new friend.

- What do you want to know about your new friend?
- What do you want to do with this friend?

1 Addresses and phone numbers

- Listen for Kim's address and phone number.

START

Friday at lunch time

Amy, can you come to my house on Saturday? We can trade stickers.

Great! I'll ask my mother. What's your phone number?

It's 279-3586.

Okay, I'll phone you tonight.

After school

Mother, I have a new friend, Kim. Can I go to her house on Saturday?

Where does Kim live?

You can phone her mother. Here's her phone number.

279-3586
Kim

KEY WORDS

stickers

279-3586
phone number

742 Laurier Street
address

Hello? Mrs. McKenzie?
This is Mrs. Woo.
I'm Amy's mother.

Hello, Mrs. Woo.
How are you?

I'm fine, thank you.
Kim invited Amy to your
house on Saturday morning.
Is it all right?

Of course.

Where do you live?

On Laurier Street.
Can Amy come?

Yes.
What's your address?

It's 742 Laurier Street.

Thank you very much,
Mrs. McKenzie.
Amy is very excited.
Goodbye.

You're welcome.
Bye.

EVERYDAY LANGUAGE

Asking About Places and Addresses:
Where do you live?

We say:
in (city)

in Rimouski
in Sherbrooke
in Montreal

We say:
on (street)

on Laurier Street
on Fourth Avenue
on Gervais Crescent

We say:
at (address)

at 742 Laurier Street
at 53 Fourth Avenue
at 1168 Gervais Crescent

② Saturday morning

GETTiNG READY TO LiSTEN AND READ

1 Look at the pictures on pages 57 to 59.
• Who does Amy meet at Kim's house?

2 Check the key words on each page.

Now listen and read along.

START

This house
is number 740.

The one with
the green door
is 742.

Hi, I'm Kim's mother.
You must be Amy.

Yes.

Hi. I'm Lee Wong,
Amy's uncle.

Hi, Amy.
I'm glad you're here.

Hi, Kim.
This is
my Uncle Lee.

Hello.
Please come in.

Pleased
to meet you.

Thank you for
inviting Amy.

🔑 KEY WORDS

house   door   uncle

KEY WORDS

kitchen   family room

Come on, Amy.
Let's look at our sticker books.

Where's your sister Lynne?

Oh, Lynne is upstairs in our bedroom. She's still asleep.

Oh, yeah. Teenagers!

STOP

KEY WORDS

upstairs
bedroom
asleep

AFTER LISTENING AND READING

1 All about the visit
- Who does Amy meet at Kim's house?
- What are Amy and Kim going to do?

2 Look at Detective Dan's Clue.
- Ask three questions about one person at the McKenzie house.

3 Make a list of things you like to do when a friend visits.

DETECTIVE DAN'S CLUE

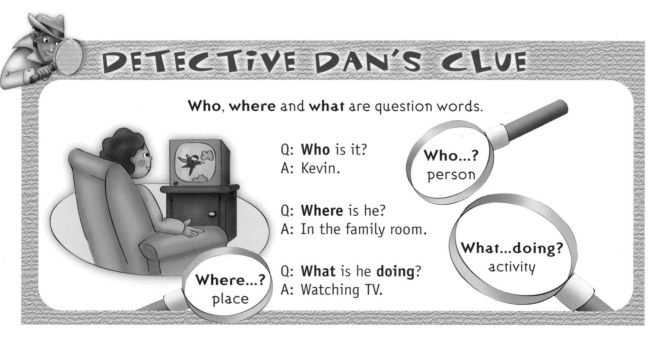

Who, **where** and **what** are question words.

Q: **Who** is it?
A: Kevin.

Who...?
person

Q: **Where** is he?
A: In the family room.

What...doing?
activity

Q: **What** is he **doing**?
A: Watching TV.

Where...?
place

I like to...
Do you?

Make a Friend!

1 Make a new friend in the class.
- Exchange addresses and phone numbers.
- Find two things you both like to do.

Examples:

play games
on the computer

read comic books

watch TV

play hockey

ride my bike

go to the park

EVERYDAY LANGUAGE

Talking About Preferences

Do you like
to...?

Yes.

I like to...

Not me.

Other ways to answer **yes**:

Of course.   *or*   **Sure.**

Ways to **agree** or **disagree**:

Yes = Me too.   *or*   **So do I.**
No = Not me.   *or*   **I don't.**

2 In small groups, put on a skit called "Meet My Friend."
- Introduce your new friend to the members of your group.
- Use the information you prepared on this page.

Amy's home
Listen.

	A	B	C
1			742
2	3021 Hillside Drive	3201 Hillside Drive	1302 Hillside Drive
3	279-4863	279-1843	279-6853

Amy's family
Listen.

- Take turns asking questions about Amy's home and her family.
- Use the question words:
  who, where, what...doing.

After this unit I can...

How are *you* doing?

STORY TIME

Enjoy a story. Your teacher will help you.

GETTING READY TO LISTEN AND READ

1 Read the title and look at the pictures.
- Predict what this story is about.

   a) living in an apartment building
   b) going to a winter carnival
   c) visiting friends

2 Look for the key words in the story.
- Match the key words with the pictures.

🔑 KEY WORDS

| apartment building | hill | snow | inner tube | toboggan |
| flying saucer | sled | race | balloon | magic carpet |

A    B    C

D   E 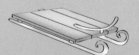   F

G    H   I

3 Look for the main character.
- What is her name?

J

Now listen and read along.

START

Natasha and Her Friends

Illustrations: Josée Morin

1 Natasha lives in an apartment building.
She lives with her father and her little sister, Marlene.

2 Natasha has many friends in the apartment building.

3 There is a big park near the apartment building.
In the park there is a hill. The hill is covered with snow.
Today is a special day. It's Winter Carnival!

4 All the children under five years old have red balloons.
All the children from six to twelve years old have green balloons.
All the other children have yellow balloons.
All the fathers have orange balloons.
All the mothers have blue balloons.

5 Toboggans, sleds, flying saucers, magic carpets
and inner tubes slide down the hill.
Look at Natasha. She's on a magic carpet.

6 Here comes Marlene. She's sliding down the hill on an inner tube.

7 Here come the flying saucers! There's Jeremy, Natasha's friend.

8 Look at Natasha's father!
He's on a toboggan.

9 It's time for the race. All the children with green balloons – on your mark, get set, go! They all race to the bottom of the hill. Who's first? It's Luke. Hurray for Luke!

AFTER LISTENING AND READING

1 Answer these questions.
a) Who wins the race?
b) Who is Natasha's friend?
c) What colour is Natasha's balloon?

2 Imagine you are at the carnival.
• What colour is your balloon?
• What would you use to slide down the hill?

3 Draw a picture of your family.
• Colour a balloon for each person.

PROJECT — Making a Poster About You and Your Friends

① Collecting information for the poster

- Write a friend's name in the middle of your planning sheet.

- Next write in the categories. Look for ideas in Units 5 and 6. These pictures are clues.

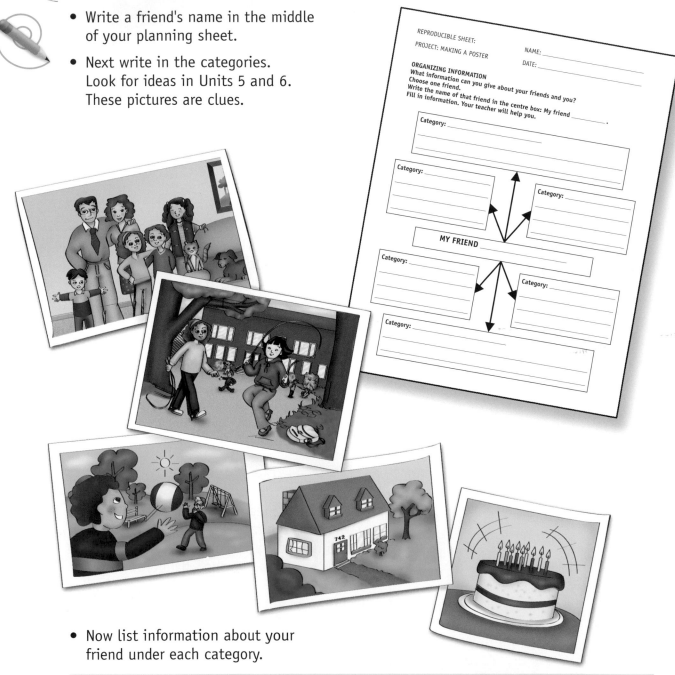

REPRODUCIBLE SHEET:

PROJECT: MAKING A POSTER

NAME: _____

DATE: _____

ORGANIZING INFORMATION
What information can you give about your friends and you?
Choose one friend.
Write the name of that friend in the centre box: My friend _____ .
Fill in information. Your teacher will help you.

Category: _____

Category: _____

Category: _____

MY FRIEND

Category: _____

Category: _____

Category: _____

- Now list information about your friend under each category.

You can write about one, two or three friends.
Prepare a planning sheet for each friend.

② Writing the information

- Look at your planning sheet.
- Circle the information you want to put on the poster.
- Write a first draft.

  1. Look for key words in *Clues* or in a dictionary.
  2. Use the correct pronouns:

he for a male　　　**she** for a female　　　**we** for you and your friend

- Read your first draft.

  1. Check your sentences for capital letters and correct punctuation.
  2. Check your sentence structure.

> subject　verb
> 　↑　　　↑
> *We collect stickers.*

3. Check for correct spelling.
4. Exchange drafts with a classmate.

YOUR PROJECT

1 Decide where you want to put the information on the poster.

2 Remember to write the title *My Friends and Me.*

3 Draw pictures of you and your friends.

4 Write the sentences.
- Remember to enter all the corrections.
- Ask your partner to check the corrections.

5 Show your poster to the class.

6 Read the information on your classmates' posters.

A Special Day

What is the special day?
• Look at the pictures.

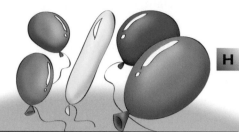

H

A

G

COME TO OUR PARTY

Date _____

Time _____

Address _____

Phone Number _____

For _____

R.S.V.P.

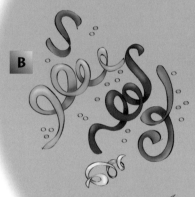

B

F

C

D

E

KEY WORDS

balloons	calendar
hats	cake
card	presents
streamers	invitation

• Name the things you do for a party.
• Match the key words with the pictures.

Look at page 80.
• What will you do at the end of this unit?
• What do you need to know to do this?

① A birthday party

GETTING READY TO LISTEN AND READ

1 Look at the pictures and answer the questions.
a) pages 71 and 72:
- Whose birthday is it?
- What are they going to eat at the party?
- What are they going to drink?

b) page 73:
- Who are these people?

c) page 75:
- Who is invited to the party?

2 Look at the key words on page 74. Find the pictures on the page.

Now listen and read along.

START It's Sunday afternoon. Kim, Kevin and their mother are planning a birthday party.

What do you want to eat at your party? Hot dogs, hamburgers, pizza?

PIZZA!

What kind of birthday cake do you want?

Chocolate with chocolate icing.

White with chocolate icing.

Okay. I'll order two large pizzas from Alberto's Pizzeria.

Two days later at Dan Martin's house

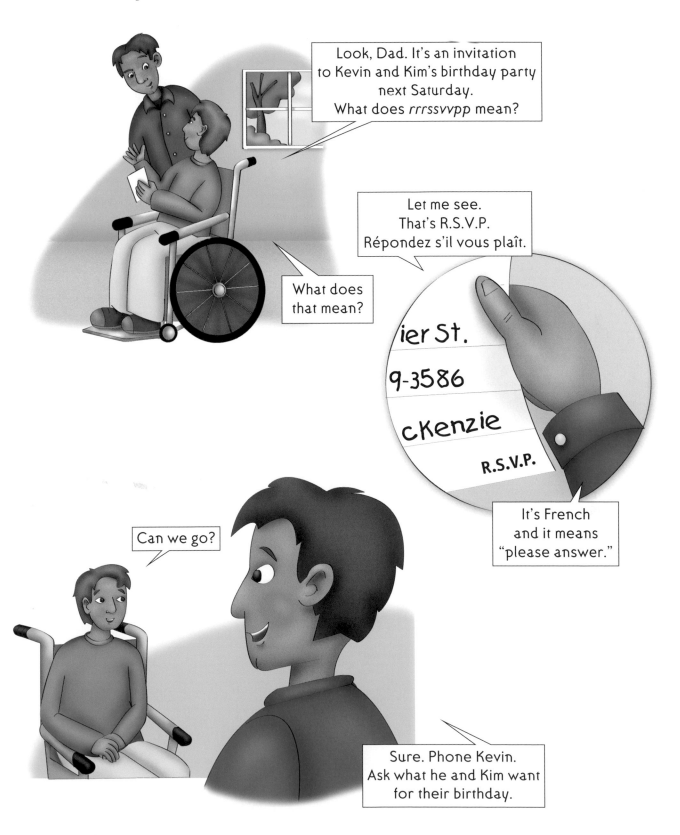

Saturday afternoon at the party

What kind of cake is it? I wanted a chocolate cake with chocolate icing.

I wanted a white cake with chocolate icing.

It's a marble cake.

That's our mom!

STOP

AFTER LISTENING AND READING

1 True or false?
a) The twins' birthday party is on May 12.
b) The birthday party is from 3:00 to 5:00 p.m.
c) Max Martin is the twins' uncle.
d) Kevin wants a bicycle for his birthday.
e) Kim wants a kite.
f) Mrs. McKenzie makes a chocolate cake for the party.

2 Imagine you are going to the twins' party.
What presents would you give Kevin and Kim?

3 What do you want for your birthday?

EVERYDAY LANGUAGE

Giving and Receiving Presents

Ways to Say "Thank You"

2 Party food and drinks

What do these girls and boys want for their birthday parties?

- Listen.

Annie   Denny   Julie   Max   Amy   Brian

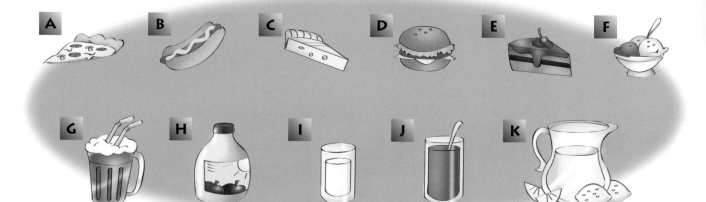

3 Birthday presents

What do these girls and boys want for their birthdays?

- Listen.

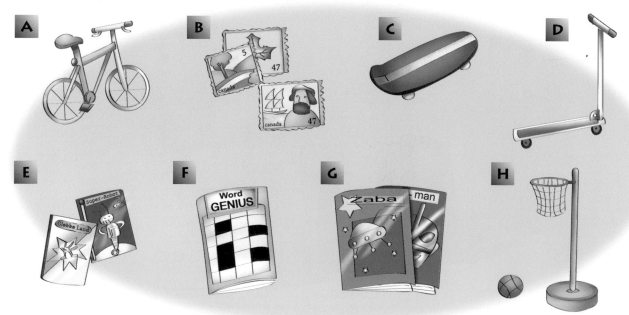

4 Talking about dates

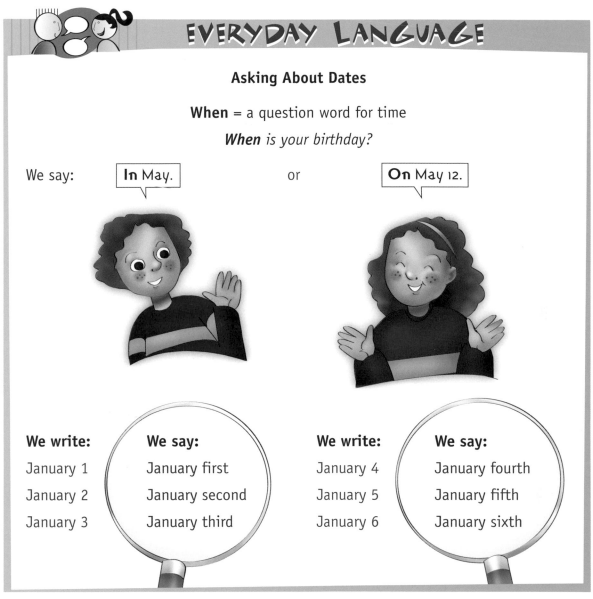

EVERYDAY LANGUAGE

Asking About Dates

When = a question word for time

When *is your birthday?*

We say: **In** May.   or   **On** May 12.

We write:	We say:	We write:	We say:
January 1	January first	January 4	January fourth
January 2	January second	January 5	January fifth
January 3	January third	January 6	January sixth

• Practice saying these dates.

A. January 10   D. February 17   G. March 8   J. April 15
B. May 30   E. June 11   H. July 12   K. August 14
C. September 20   F. October 19   I. November 24 L. December 31

5 A class birthday survey

Your teacher will give you the survey.
• Ask your classmates:
  "When is your birthday?"

Talk About Your Birthday

1 Answer the questions.

- When is your birthday?

- What do you want to eat on your birthday?

- What do you want to drink?

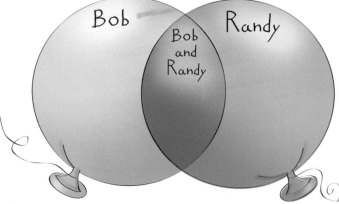

- What presents do you want?

2 Compare answers.

- Complete the diagram.
- Your teacher will explain.

Bob

Bob and Randy

Randy

3 Plan an unbirthday party.

Your teacher will explain the following:

- Make a class invitation.
- Make a party hat.
- Make an unbirthday card for a classmate.
- Play party games.

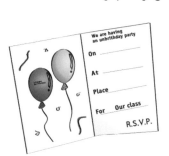

TIME OUT

The birthday party
Listen.

A

B

C

D

E

F

Tell four classmates...

- when your birthday is
- what you want to eat
- what you want to drink
- what present you want

Use complete sentences.

After this unit I can...

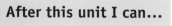

How are *you* doing?

Star light, star bright,
First star I see tonight.
I wish I may, I wish I might,
Have the wish I wish tonight.

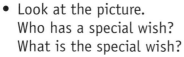

- Look at the picture.
  Who has a special wish?
  What is the special wish?

- Listen to the poem.

At the end of this unit you will write riddles about your favourite animal.

- What do you need to know to do this?

STORY TIME

Enjoy a story. Your teacher will help you.

GETTING READY TO LISTEN AND READ

1 Read the title on page 84. Look at the pictures in the story.
What is the special wish?
a) A boy wishes for money.
b) A boy wishes for many animals.
c) A boy wishes for a puppy.

2 Who is this boy?
Find his name on page 84.

3 Look for the key words in the story.
Find the pictures for the key words.

🔑 KEY WORDS

Page 84:	SPCA	dog	puppy
Page 85:	bedroom	picture	
	bank book	money	
	piggy bank	wallet	
Page 86:	idea	allowance	
Page 87:	babysit	wash	mow
Page 88:	posters	bookstore	
Page 89:	grocery store	video store	cat
Page 90:	yard		

Now listen and read along.

A Special Wish

START

1 One day Denny, his sister Debbie and his brother Justin visit the SPCA. They look at all the dogs.

2 Justin sees a cute puppy. He likes it very much. It costs $120 to adopt a dog from the SPCA.

3 That night in his bedroom, Justin draws the puppy. He puts the picture on the wall. He wants the puppy very much.

4 Justin looks in his bank book. He has $45. He counts the money in his piggy bank. He has $12.

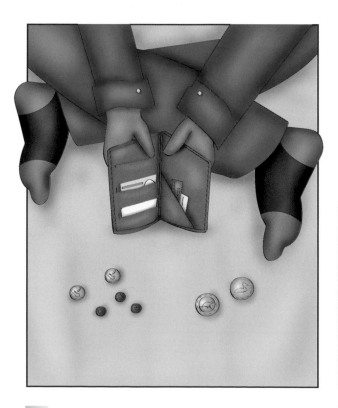

5 He counts the money in his wallet. He has just $3.53.

6 He needs $59.47.

7 Suddenly Justin has an idea.
He decides to go talk to his parents.

8 "Mom, Dad," he says. "I saw a cute puppy today. I wish I could get it. Can I, please?"

9 "Well... how much is it?" asks his stepmother.
"It's $120," answers Justin.
"Do you have $120?" asks his father.
"No, I have just $60.53," replies Justin.

10 Justin asks his parents for an advance on his allowance. His dad gives him $20.

11 Justin is sad. He still needs $39.47.

12 His stepmother makes a suggestion. "Maybe you can make some money," she says.

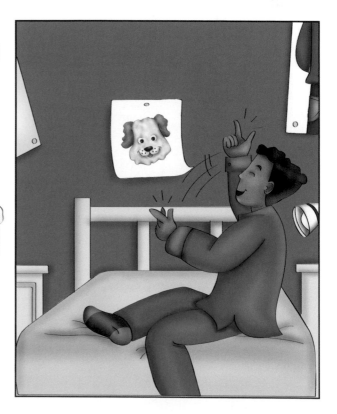

13 "You can babysit, wash cars, mow lawns or walk the neighbour's dog."

14 "Justin goes back to his bedroom. He thinks. He has another idea. He is not going to babysit. He is going to animal-sit!

15 Justin starts making posters.

16 The next day he goes to Main Street.

17 Mrs. Murphy puts up a poster in the bookstore.

18 Justin puts one in the grocery store and another in the video store.

19 On Friday night Justin gets his first phone call. A woman asks Justin to take care of a cat for the weekend.

20 Justin goes to get the pet right away. He carries the cat and some cat food home.

21 Later that night Justin gets another call. This time it's for a dog.

Will Justin's wish come true?
What do you think?

22 By Saturday afternoon, the yard is full of animals. Justin is excited. "Mom, Dad! This is fantastic!" he cries.

AFTER LISTENING AND READING

1 Will Justin's wish come true?
- Total the amounts of money Justin has.

A. How much does he have in the bank?

B. How much does he have in his piggy bank?

C. How much does he have in his wallet?

D. How much do his parents advance him?

ANIMAL-SITTING
Going away for the weekend?
Leave your pet in good hands.
Call Justin
842-3657
$2.⁰⁰ a day!

E. How much will Justin earn animal-sitting?

Count the number of animals on page 90.
Multiply the number of animals by 2.
This is how much Justin will earn.

F. How much is the puppy?

G. Does Justin have enough money to buy the puppy?
Total **A + B + C + D + E** to find out.

2 Write an ending for this story. Draw a picture of the ending.
- Share your ending with your classmates.

3 Do you have a wish?
- Draw a picture of your wish.
- Write one or two sentences about your wish.

① Describing animals

DETECTIVE DAN'S CLUE

It is a pronoun for animals, things or places.

> A monkey is funny.
> It lives in a tree.

• Learn these words.

funny

cute

gentle

fat

skinny

small

long

big

slow

fast

• Practice describing animals. Use these pictures.

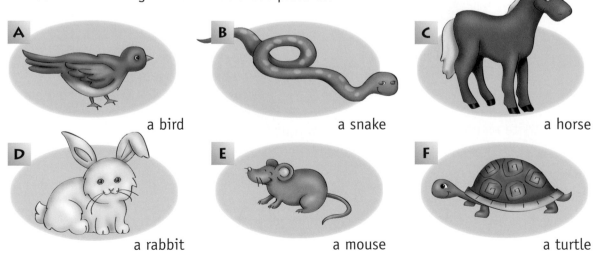

A a bird

B a snake

C a horse

D a rabbit

E a mouse

F a turtle

2 What animal is it?

Listen.

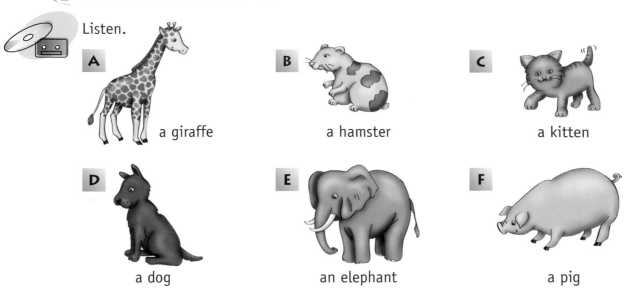

A a giraffe

B a hamster

C a kitten

D a dog

E an elephant

F a pig

3 More about animals

Your teacher will explain.

A It is pink.

B It is fat.

C It has a flat nose.

D It has a short tail.

What is it?

Describe Your Favourite Animal

My favourite animal is a rabbit.

It is gentle.

It is all white.

It moves fast.

Its name is Rapido.

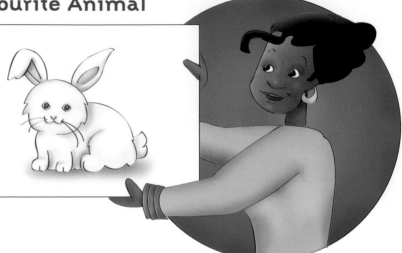

1 Draw a picture of your favourite animal.

2 Write the key words for the description on your drawing.
- What colour is it?
- What does it look like? Is it...?
  big   small   skinny   fat   etc.
- Is the animal...?
  funny   gentle   cute   fast   slow   etc.

3 Write a short description.
- Check your work for
  → correct spelling
  → complete sentences
  → capital letters
  → punctuation

4 Describe your favourite animal to your classmates.

The pet shop

Listen.

- Describe two animals on this page.
- Say three things about each animal.

How are *you* doing?

After this unit I can...

Making an Imaginary Zoo

A zoo is a place where wild animals live.
In some zoos you can see reptiles and fish, too.
People like to visit zoos.
Can you name a zoo in your area?
What animals can we see at this zoo?

YOUR PROJECT

① Plan an imaginary zoo

- As a class decide on the different sections in this imaginary zoo.

Jungle Animals   **Birds**   **Small Animals**

② Share the work

- Your teacher will explain.

- Write a short description.
  Example: "This animal will have the body of a giraffe and the head of a pig."

③ Make the imaginary animal

- Use the description you prepared with your team.
- Name the animal.

This is a Girig.

④ As a team...

- assemble your section of the zoo.
- show it to the class.
- describe your animal to your classmates.

ALL YEAR ROUND

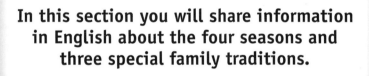

In this section you will share information in English about the four seasons and three special family traditions.

What do you know about the seasons?

- Answer these questions.
    1. What season begins on December 21 and ends March 19?
    2. What season begins on September 22 and ends December 20?
    3. What season begins on June 21 and ends September 21?
    4. What season begins on March 20 and ends June 20?

- Make an All Year Round key word web.
    1. Form groups of four.
    2. Decide who will do *fall*, *winter*, *spring* and *summer*.
    3. Use the following categories:
       clothing, *colours*, *special events*, *activities* and *the weather*.
    4. Find some of the key words in this unit.

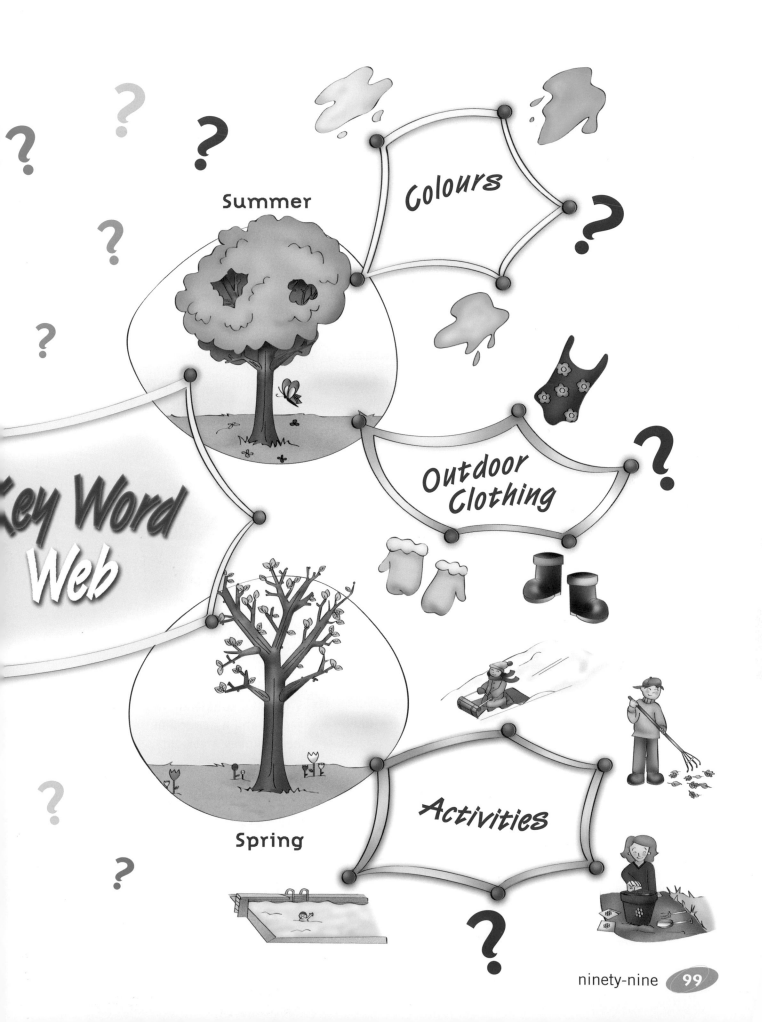

Summer

Colours

Outdoor
Clothing

Key Word
Web

Spring

Activities

Fall Fun
At the McKenzies'

START

A It's fall. The leaves change colour. They turn yellow, red, orange and brown. When the leaves fall, Kevin and Kim rake them.

B Kim, Kevin and Rusty like to play in the leaves. Kevin likes to jump in the leaves. Rusty, too.

C The twins pick apples, too. This is Kim's favourite fall activity.

D When it's cold, they wear a sweater or jacket and a cap. Sometimes they need gloves and boots.

KEY WORDS

leaves   rake   jump   pick

E Thanksgiving is a special holiday in October. It's the second Monday in October. October 31 is a special day, too. It's Halloween!

F The first snowfall is usually in the fall. Sometimes it is in October; sometimes it is in November.

Make a Fall Class Book

1. Draw pictures of your favourite things about fall. Write a sentence under each picture.

2. Share your pictures with your classmates. Make a class book.

I like to pick apples.

I like to jump in the leaves.

Winter Fun

What is your favourite activity on this page?

Dog sledding

Looking at snow sculptures at the winter carnival in Quebec City

Skating on the Rideau Canal in Ottawa

Going on a sleigh ride

Ice fishing

Barrel jumping

A beautiful, sunny, winter day

- Find three fun activities on this page.
- Find the words for the activities on this page and page 104.
- Listen to the poem.

SNOW FUN

Snowflakes are falling,
Winter has begun.
Let's go out
And have some fun.

Let's build a snowman,
Throw snowballs, too.
Let's run hand in hand,
Me and you.

Zakera Jafar, age 9

KEY WORDS

snowflakes

snowman

snowballs

Kim and Kevin have fun in winter with their friends.

START

1 When it snows they make a big snowman.

2 Kim likes to make snow angels.

3 Kevin and his friends make snow forts and have snowball fights.

4 Winter sports are fun. The kids play hockey.

5 They go tobogganing...

6 sledding...

7 and skating.

STOP

Compare Your Preferences

- Compare what you like and don't like about winter.
- Make a diagram like Kim and Kevin's.

Talking About Preferences

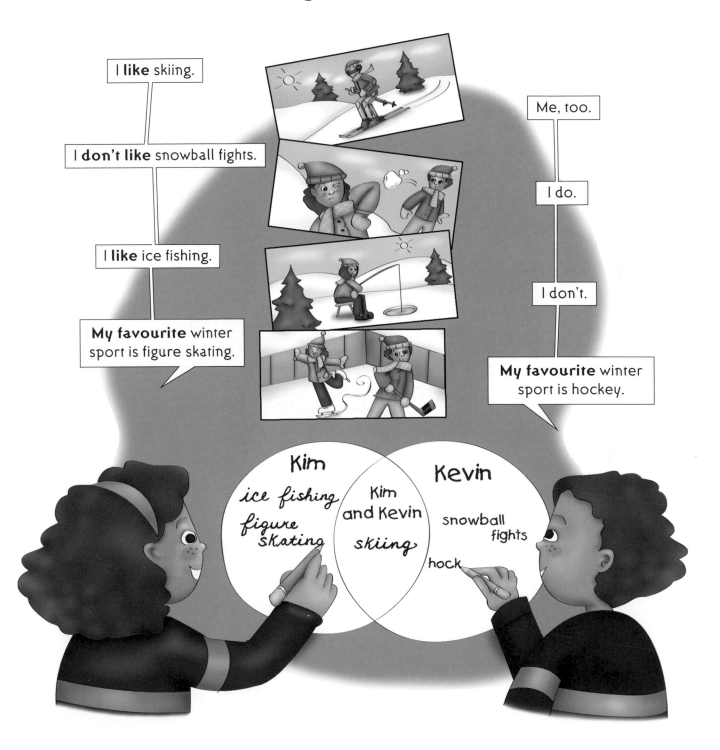

Spring Clean-up

The students in Elementary 4 at North Elementary School made these posters.

NORTH ELEMENTARY SCHOOL

SPRING CLEAN-UP MAY 15

Spring Clean-up

BE PROUD OF YOUR SCHOOL

PLANT FLOWERS

DON'T LITTER

- Find the key words on the posters.

Are these sentences true or false?
a) It is spring.
b) The students decided to clean up the schoolyard.
c) The date of the clean-up is June 15.

KEY WORDS

clean-up

litter

proud

plant flowers

START How did the students clean up the schoolyard? Listen.

The students in Elementary 4 decided to make spring clean-up a class project. They invited the whole school to join. On May 15 all the students at North Elementary met in the schoolyard.

They picked up all the litter.

They planted trees and flowers.

They collected cans and bottles.

Everyone was very proud when the clean-up was finished.

STOP

KEY WORDS

pick up   plant   collect

YOU'RE ON

Plan a Clean-Up Project

Does your schoolyard look like North Elementary's yard before the clean-up?
- Plan a clean-up project with your teacher.
- Make posters. Get the whole school to help.

or

Make the Mini-Booklet *Pete's Clean-Up*

Pete's Clean-Up

Summer Holidays

Different people, different holidays – do you do any of these activities?

- Find the key words in the headings.

A Having a picnic

In Saint-Zotique, Quebec

B Going to country fairs and festivals

Western Festival in Saint-Tite, Quebec

C Visiting the zoo

The Metro Toronto Zoo

D Playing at the beach

Lake Huron, Ontario

E Swimming at the pool

A public swimming pool in Vancouver

F Going camping

In Saint-Félicien, Quebec

KEY WORDS

picnic	country fair	festival	zoo	beach
pool	camping	swimming	playing	visiting

Listen to what Kim, Kevin and their friends like to do in the summer.

A

I like to go camping.

B

Yeah, I like camping, too, but playing on the beach is the greatest!

C

I like to visit my cousin in Toronto and go to the zoo.

D

I like to take swimming lessons at the pool. This summer I want to learn how to dive.

E

Every summer we go to our cottage. I like to go fishing with my dad.

F

We stay at home in the summer. I like to play at the park and go bicycling with my friends.

G

I visit my grandparents on the reserve. I like playing with my cousins.

KEY WORDS

cousin	lessons
dive	cottage
fishing	bicycling

What do your classmates like to do in the summer?

- Do a class survey. Ask: *"What is your favourite summer activity?"*
- Find out who...

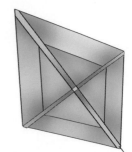

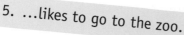

1. ...likes to go camping.

2. ...likes to go fishing.

3. ...likes to go to fairs.

4. ...likes to go on picnics.

5. ...likes to go to the zoo.

6. ...likes to go to the pool.

7. ...likes to go to the beach.

8. ...likes to [????]

9. ...likes to [????]

10. ...likes to [????]

What is the most popular activity?

YOU'RE ON

Share Your Summer Plans

- Write a short description.

This summer I am going to ...

1 Check your sentences.
- Does the first word in the sentence begin with a capital?
- Does each sentence end with a period?

2 Ask a classmate to check your description.

3 Write your final draft.
- Decorate your description.
- Share the information with your classmates.

HALLOWEEN

 Listen to the poem.

PUMPKIN

We bought a fat orange pumpkin,
The plumpest sort they sell.
We neatly scooped the inside out
And only left the shell.

We carved a funny, funny-face
Of silly shape and size,
A pointy nose, a jagged mouth
And two enormous eyes.

We set it in a window
And we put a candle in,
Then lit it up for all to see
Our jack-o'-lantern grin.

Jack Prelutsky

- Find the key words in the pictures and in the poem.

KEY WORDS

pumpkin
jack-o'-lantern
face
nose
mouth
eye
window

scooped

shell

candle

Talk About Your Halloween

1. Does your family have a jack-o'-lantern at Halloween?
   - Draw a picture of your jack-o'-lantern.
   - Show it to your group.

2. Where do you put the jack-o'-lantern?

3. What is your costume?

4. What kinds of treats does your family give out?

5. What do you **like** or **not like** about Halloween?

Christmas and New Year's

Does your family celebrate Christmas and New Year's?

• Find out what different families do.

1 CHRISTMAS WITH THE MCKENZIES

START ### Getting ready for Christmas

A

The family decorates the Christmas tree.
Mr. McKenzie puts the lights on the tree.
Mrs. McKenzie and the children decorate
it with ornaments.

B

> I want a train set,
> a teddy bear and a wagon.

Dear Santa,
Here is my
Christmas list.
I want a train,
a teddy bear and
a wagon.
I have been
good.

Robert McK

> Good.
> Now listen to the letter.

Lynne helps Robert write a letter to
Santa Claus.

C

Mrs. McKenzie and Lynne bake special
Christmas cookies.

D

Mr. McKenzie wraps the Christmas presents.

KEY WORDS

Christmas tree   letter   Santa Claus   cookies   presents   wraps

Christmas Eve

On Christmas Eve, the family goes to church.

The children put out their Christmas stockings. Robert leaves milk and cookies for Santa Claus.

Christmas Day

On Christmas morning everyone opens their presents.

In the afternoon the McKenzie family goes to Grandma and Grandpa Wilson's for Christmas dinner.

KEY WORDS

church

stockings

milk

dinner

For your presentation
Prepare information about your family traditions...

Does your family have the same traditions as the McKenzie family?
• Write about your family traditions.

2 NEW YEAR'S WITH THE WOOS

What two activities are similar to the McKenzies'?
What activities are similar to yours?
Listen.

 **START** The Woos celebrate Chinese New Year.
It falls in January or February.

A

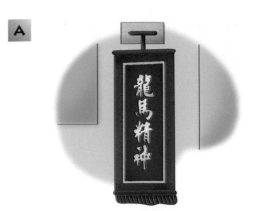

The Woos hang up messages of good luck.

B

On New Year's Eve they have a special dinner with their family and friends.

C

Children receive red envelopes called
lai see. In the *lai see* there is money.

D

On New Year's Day there is
a Lion Dance.

 STOP

 **KEY WORDS**

messages

good luck

lai see

envelopes

money

Lion Dance

For your presentation
Prepare information about your family traditions...

Does your family have any other traditions?
- Write them down.
- Ask your teacher for help.

3 CELEBRATIONS IN NATIVE COMMUNITIES

Where do these celebrations take place? Listen.

START In northern Quebec, Inuit communities celebrate Christmas with many events and games.

In Inukjuak, elementary students put on a Christmas pageant.

KEY WORDS

igloo

pageant

In Povungnituk, the natives have an igloo-building contest. STOP

YOU'RE ON

Share Your Holiday Activities

1 Prepare your presentation.

A
- Draw your Christmas tree or other decorations.
- Write a short description.

B
- Draw a picture of other special activities.
- Write a sentence or two about each activity.
- Circle your favourite activity in your favourite colour.

2 Sing Christmas songs.

Valentine's Day

The McKenzies celebrate Valentine's Day.

1

Mr. McKenzie buys Valentine treats for everyone.

2

Mrs. McKenzie makes special heart-shaped chocolate chip cookies.

3

The children make Valentine cards for their parents and their grandparents.

4

Kim and Kevin make Valentine cards for their friends, too.

YOU'RE ON

Exchange English Valentine Cards

- Write your name on a piece of paper.
- Put all of the names into a bag.
- Take turns pulling out a name.
- Make a Valentine card for that person.

SONGS

It's School Time

Chorus spoken

It's school time,
It's school time.
Can you tell me what time it is?
It's time for school.

1. Let's go to the classroom,
   Let's go to the classroom.
   Put away your ruler,
   Put away your pencil,
   Take your scissors,
   Take your glue.
   That's what we do in the classroom.

Chorus sung

2. Let's go to the gym,
   Let's go to the gym.
   Put on your running shoes,
   Put on your T-shirt,
   Bring the ball
   And bring the net.
   That's what we do in the gym.

Chorus sung

3. Let's go to the library,
   Let's go to the library.
   Take out a new book,
   Go to the front desk,
   Show your card,
   Don't talk too loud.
   That's what we do in the library.

Chorus sung twice

COLOURS AND SHAPES

1. We see all kinds of shapes,
    We see all kinds of colours.
    It's fun to know our shapes.
    It's fun to know our colours.

2. Red is a colour, red is a colour,
    Red is the colour of a stop sign.
    Green is a colour, green is a colour,
    Green is the colour of the leaves in the trees.

3. Yellow is a colour, yellow is a colour,
    Yellow is the colour of a lemon pie.
    Blue is a colour, blue is a colour,
    Blue is the colour of the bright blue sky.

4. White is a colour, white is a colour,
    White is the colour of the moon at night.
    We have pink, orange, purple and brown
    But it's black when we turn off the lights.

5. Everybody in red,
    Stand up.
    Everybody in green,
    Stand up.
    Everybody turn right then left.
    Now everybody sit down.

6. Square is a shape,
    SQUARE IS A SHAPE.
    Square is a shape that we use for a box.
    Rectangle is a shape,
    RECTANGLE IS A SHAPE.
    Rectangle is a shape that we use for a door.

7. Triangle is a shape,
    TRIANGLE IS A SHAPE.
    Triangle is a great big pyramid.
    Circle is a shape.
    CIRCLE IS A SHAPE.
    A circle is the shape of the sun.

8. Everybody in yellow,
    STAND UP.
    Everybody in blue,
    STAND UP.
    Everybody turn right then left.
    Now everybody sit down.

    Repeat the last verse

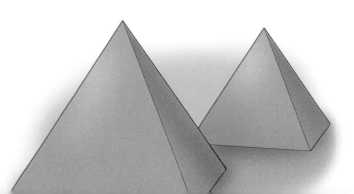

The Robot Song

1. Let's all walk like a robot!
   Then tell me how a robot walks.
   Well, it's forward and back
   With a clunketty-clack.
   That's how a robot walks.
   That's how a robot walks.

Clunketty-clack

3. Let's all sing like a robot!
   Then tell me how a robot sings.
   It's a very short song
   That goes bonketty-bong.
   That's how a robot sings.
   That's how a robot sings.

Bonketty-bong

2. Let's all talk like a robot!
   Then tell me how a robot talks.
   Well, it's ticketty-tick
   And a clicketty-click.
   That's how a robot talks.
   That's how a robot talks.

Ticketty-tick

4. So together go clunketty-clack.
   And together go ticketty-tick.
   Sing a very short song
   That goes bonketty-bong
   And together go clicketty-click.
   And together go clicketty-click.

This Old Man

This old man, he played one,
He played knick-knack on my thumb!
With a knick-knack paddywhack,
Give a dog a bone,
This old man came rolling home.

This old man, he played two,
He played knick-knack on my shoe!
With a knick-knack paddywhack,
Give a dog a bone,
This old man came rolling home.

This old man, he played three,
He played knick-knack on my knee!
With a knick-knack paddywhack,
Give a dog a bone,
This old man came rolling home.

This old man, he played four,
He played knick-knack on my door!
With a knick-knack paddywhack,
Give a dog a bone,
This old man came rolling home.

This old man, he played five,
He played knick-knack on my hive!
With a knick-knack paddywhack,
Give a dog a bone,
This old man came rolling home.

This old man, he played six,
He played knick-knack on my sticks!
With a knick-knack paddywhack,
Give a dog a bone,
This old man came rolling home.

This old man, he played seven,
He played knick-knack up in heaven!
With a knick-knack paddywhack,
Give a dog a bone,
This old man came rolling home.

This old man, he played eight,
He played knick-knack on my gate!
With a knick-knack paddywhack,
Give a dog a bone,
This old man came rolling home.

This old man, he played nine,
He played knick-knack on my spine!
With a knick-knack paddywhack,
Give a dog a bone,
This old man came rolling home.

This old man, he played ten
He played knick-knack once again!
With a knick-knack paddywhack,
Give a dog a bone,
This old man came rolling home.

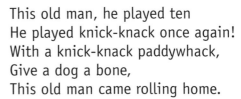

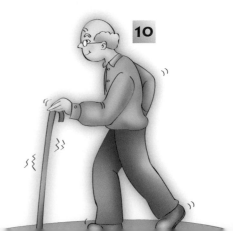

A-Hunting We Will Go

A-hunting we will go, a-hunting we will go,
Heigh-ho, the derry-o, a-hunting we will go.
A-hunting we will go, a-hunting we will go,
We'll catch a fox and put it in a box
And then we'll let it go.

A-hunting we will go, a-hunting we will go,
Heigh-ho, the derry-o, a-hunting we will go.
A-hunting we will go, a-hunting we will go,
We'll catch a fish and put it in a dish
And then we'll let it go.

A-hunting we will go, a-hunting we will go,
Heigh-ho, the derry-o, a-hunting we will go.
A-hunting we will go, a-hunting we will go,
We'll catch a bear and cut its hair
And then we'll let it go.

A-hunting we will go, a-hunting we will go,
Heigh-ho, the derry-o, a-hunting we will go.
A-hunting we will go, a-hunting we will go,
We'll catch a pig and dance a jig
And then we'll let it go.

A-hunting we will go, a-hunting we will go,
Heigh-ho, the derry-o, a-hunting we will go.
A-hunting we will go, a-hunting we will go,
We'll catch a giraffe and make it laugh
And then we'll let it go.

It's Wintertime

It's wintertime.
It's wintertime.

Play hockey,
Go skating,
Make snowballs
And have some fun!

It's cold out there.
It's cold out there.

Put on a coat,
Put on a tuque,
Put on your boots
And have some fun!

It's freezing out there.
It's freezing out there.

Wear gloves,
Wear mittens,
Wear a scarf
And have some fun!

It's snowing out there.
It's snowing out there.

Make a fort,
Make an angel!
Make a snowman
And have some fun!

It's wintertime.
It's wintertime.

Play hockey,
Go skating,
Make snowballs
And have some fun!

The Recycling Boogie

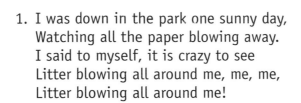

1. I was down in the park one sunny day,
   Watching all the paper blowing away.
   I said to myself, it is crazy to see
   Litter blowing all around me, me, me,
   Litter blowing all around me!

2. So pick up your paper, recycle it too.
   Don't be a litterbug, it's so uncool.
   Save that plastic, round up the cans.
   Be proud to clean up your land, land, land,
   Proud to clean up your land.
   Be proud to clean up your land, land, land,
   Proud to clean up your land.

3. Pick up your bottles, recycle them too.
   Don't be a litterbug, it's so uncool,
   Save that plastic, round up the cans.
   Be proud to clean up your land, land, land,
   Proud to clean up your land.
   Be proud to clean up your land, land, land,
   Proud to clean up your land.

4. Get back home and what do I see?
   There's garbage hanging in my very own tree.
   Wherever I turn, wherever I go,
   There's garbage flying high and low, low, low,
   Garbage flying high and low!

5. So pick up your garbage, recycle it too.
   Don't be a litterbug, it's so uncool,
   Save that plastic, round up the cans.
   Be proud to clean up your land, land, land,
   Proud to clean up your land.
   Be proud to clean up your land, land, land,
   Proud to clean up your land.

Up on the Rooftop

Up on the rooftop reindeer pause,
Out jumps good old Santa Claus!
Down through the chimney with lots of toys,
All for the little ones, Christmas joys.

Chorus
Ho, ho, ho! Who wouldn't go?
Ho, ho, ho! Who wouldn't go?
Up on the rooftop, click, click, click,
Down through the chimney
With good Saint Nick!

First comes the stocking of little Nell
Oh, dear Santa fill it well!
Give her a dolly that laughs and cries,
One that will open and shut her eyes.

Chorus

Look in the stocking of little Will.
Oh, just see what a glorious fill!
Here is a hammer and lots of tacks,
Whistle and ball and a whip that cracks!

Chorus

We Wish You a Merry Christmas

Chorus

We wish you a merry Christmas,
We wish you a merry Christmas,
We wish you a merry Christmas
And a happy new year.
Good tidings to you and all of your kin,
We wish you a merry Christmas
And a happy new year.

1. Now bring us some Christmas pudding,
   Now bring us some Christmas pudding,
   Now bring us some Christmas pudding,
   Now bring us some right here.

   Sing chorus

2. And we won't go until we get some,
   And we won't go until we get some,
   And we won't go until we get some,
   So bring some right here.

   Sing chorus

REFERENCES

1 COURTEOUS EXPRESSIONS

Saying "Hello"
Hello.
Hi.
Good morning.
Good afternoon.
Good evening.

Saying "Goodbye"
Goodbye.
Bye.
So long.
See you.
See you tomorrow.

Saying "Thank you"
Thank you.
Thanks.
Thank you very much.
Thanks a lot.

Apologizing
I'm sorry.
Sorry.
Excuse me.

Being polite
Please.

2 AGREEING AND DISAGREEING

Saying "Yes"	Saying "No"
Yes.	No.
Okay.	No way.
Sure.	Not me.
Right.	Not that.
All right.	I don't think so.
That's right.	Never.
Me too.	I don't agree.
Certainly.	
Of course.	

Expressing uncertainty
Maybe.   I'm not sure.

3 ASKING FOR CLARIFICATION

Repeat that, please.
Say that again, please.
I don't understand.
How do you say *fille* in English?
How do you spell "school"?

4 INSTRUCTIONS AND COMMANDS

Stand up.	Open your book.
Sit down.	Close your desk.
Come here.	Go to the board.

Give me your book.
Pass out the papers.

5 PERMISSION

Can I go to
the washroom?

May I sharpen
my pencil?

6 PREFERENCES

I like soccer.   **I don't like** baseball.   **My favourite** winter sport is snowboarding.

7 ASKING FOR HELP

Help me, please.
Can you help me, please?
I need help.

8 ASKING FOR MORE TIME

Wait.
Hold it.
One minute.
Wait a minute.
Just one minute.

9 OFFERING HELP

Can I help?
Can I help you?
Can I erase the board?

10 WARNINGS

Watch out!
Look out!
Be careful.

11 SUGGESTIONS

Let's play cards.
Do you want to play cards?
Want to play cards?

12 EXPRESSING FEELINGS

I'm happy.   I'm sad.

I'm mad.   I'm nervous.
I'm angry.

13 ENCOURAGEMENT

Good idea!   Great idea!
I like that.   Super.
You're a genius.   You're brilliant!

14 INVITATIONS

Come to my house.   Come over after lunch.
Can you come to my house?   Can you come?
Do you want to come to my house?   Want to come to my house?

DETECTiVE DAN'S CLUES

CLUE 1 — Talking about location

The rabbit is **in** the hat. The rabbit is **on** the hat. The rabbit is **under** the hat.

CLUE 2 — Using possessives: *my, her, his*

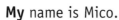

My name is Mico. **Her** name is Kim. **His** name is Kevin.

CLUE 3 — Using pronouns: *I, you, he, she, it*

I am a detective. **You** are a robot.

He is a student. **She** is a magician. **It** is a rabbit.

CLUE 4 — Using adjectives

long	hair
adjective	noun

She has long hair.
Her hair is long.

short	hair
adjective	noun

He has short hair.
His hair is short.

DETECTIVE DAN'S CLUES

CLUE 5 — Using regular verbs in the present tense

I **play** soccer.

You **play** soccer.

For the pronouns **he** and **she**, add an **s** to the verb.

He play**s** soccer.   **She** play**s** soccer.

CLUE 6 — Asking for information (question words)

Questions   **Answers**

1. Use *who* for a person.
   Who is that?   My mother.

2. Use *what* for an object.
   What is it?   A book.

3. Use *where* for a place.
   Where is it?   On my desk.

4. Use *what...doing* for an activity.
   What is she **doing**?   Watching T.V.

5. Use *whose* for possession.
   Whose lunch bag is this?   It's Detective Dan's.

6. Use *how old* for age.   Ten.
   How old are you?   I'm ten.
                                                I'm ten years old.

Yes/No questions   **Answers**

1. **Are** you nine years old?   Yes. *or* Yes, I am.   No. *or* No, I'm not.
2. **Is** he your brother?   Yes. *or* Yes, he is.   No. *or* No, he's not.
3. **Do** you have a sister?   Yes. *or* Yes, I do.   No. *or* No, I don't.
4. **Does** she go to school?   Yes. *or* Yes, she does.   No. *or* No, she doesn't.
5. **Can** I have pizza?   Yes. *or* Yes, you can.   No. *or* No, you can't.

LEARNING STRATEGIES

For reading

Strategy 1 Look at the pictures. Get an idea of the content.

Strategy 2 Look for familiar words.

Strategy 3 Learn the key words.

For writing

Strategy 1 Organize your work.
- Prepare some ideas.
- Use references.

Examples: Clues a dictionary the Internet

- Write a first draft.

Strategy 2 Check your work.
- **Spelling** s~~c~~ool ⟶ school

- **Sentences** Mico   is   a robot.
  subject verb

- **Capital letters**
  - Use a capital letter for the **first word** in the sentence.
    Example: The children like to play soccer.
    capital letter

  - Use a capital letter for **names** and the pronoun "**I**".
    Example: Kevin and I are twins.

- **Punctuation** Mico can tidy desks**.**   Can Mico tidy desks**?**
  a period a question mark

- **Ask for help.**

Strategy 3 Write a final draft.
- Check all your corrections.